THE LOVE OF THE INK: A BOOK ABOUT FOUNTAIN PENS

FOR BEGINNERS: LEARN ALL ABOUT FOUNTAIN PENS IN ONE DAY

HARRISON WEST

TABLE OF CONTENTS

WHY I WROTE THIS BOOK

It's said that the pen is mightier than the sword, but I like to think that, when you wield a fountain pen, you upgrade from a sword to a full on army. There is a gracefulness to writing with this particular implement and I think it is an art that is often overlooked—it's just plain awesome.

Our busy lives encourage us to leave messages that are short and to the point. All our mail seems to be electronic, but the joy of receiving a hand-written letter or invitation that is written in real ink and on quality paper is more satisfying than a missive on social media. There is a myth that owning a fountain pen is a costly business and, with this book, I am about to show you the best way to regain a dying art and improves your penmanship. Let me help you understand the art & beauty of fountain pens...

WHY YOU SHOULD READ THIS BOOK

Some of the most prestigious signatures in the world have been signed using a fountain pen, but do we all know how they work? How does the ink arrive at the nib? Do they need maintenance and cleaning? If these are questions that have prevented you from trying out your first fountain pen, you can find the answers here.

I'll teach you all about the art of pens so that you can use, understand, enjoy & select the best pen for you.

Maybe you used a fountain pen when you were younger and miss the elegance of the smooth strokes you can achieve. Ballpoint pens have their uses, but this book will show you that you can write with a fountain pen for everyday use.

Read this book and prepare to enter the world of the fountain pen and all that it entails.

CHAPTER ONE: THE HISTORY OF THE FOUNTAIN PEN

Picture the scene: the year is 1883, and we are in the office of a businessman in New York City with Lewis Waterman, a high-flying insurance broker, who is preparing to sign a contract that will change his future.

He has marked the occasion with the purchase of a new fountain pen. He proudly takes out his new pen and hands it to his potential new client to sign the contract with a flourish. Horror of horrors, the pen refuses to work. Worse still, it leaks all over the new contract...and renders it useless.

The horrified Waterman rushes back to his own office to obtain a new copy of the contract, but a quick-thinking competitor swoops in and steals the business instead!

Humiliated, and feeling that he is the butt of a joke among his fellow brokers, he resolves to make sure he never faces such ignominy again. He began to make fountain pens in the workshop that his brother owned.

The Early Fountain Pens

Writing instruments that carried their own ink supplies were not a new concept. In fact, the idea had been around for a century before that fateful day in New York. Waterman was intent on improving the existing concept in order to improve quality in writing implements.

Quills that were made from birds' feathers inspired early inventors as there seemed to be a natural reserve in the hollow channel of the feather. Early models tried to emulate this channel and developed into pens that did not need to be dipped into the inkwell constantly. However, a feather is not the perfect model for a pen.

Early versions consisted of a long narrow reservoir made of hard rubber with a nib on the end. Although this was a step forward, they were still a long way away from a smooth writing instrument that contained its own ink supply.

History suggests that the oldest form of fountain pen that was successfully marketed was a model made in 1702, and produced by a Frenchman named M. Bion. There are still working versions of this original model in use today.

A century later, there was a flurry of activity in the pen making world as a shoemaker from Baltimore named Williamson received the first ever patent in US history to produce his version of the fountain pen.

The British followed suit ten years later and awarded a patent to one John Schaeffer. His version of the pen was the first to be mass manufactured, as previous versions were handcrafted or used simple machinery to produce them. Then, in 1831, John Parker filed a patent for the first self-filling pen to hit the market.

These were the alternatives available to Waterman at the time and they were all plagued by ink spills and other imperfections that made them difficult to market. This simple botch up over a contract led Waterman to design a pen that would be more efficient and practical. It would change the face of fountain pens forever.

The Waterman Pen

Waterman began work on his first pen and used the capillarity principle to steady the flow of ink and make the pen write in a smooth, trouble-free way. He revolutionized the nib design by adding an air hole to it. He further improved the pen by adding a series of grooves to the feed section of the pen. With his new creation ready to hit the market he applied for a patent in 1884 and christened his pen "The Regular" decorated it with wooden accents and preceded to sell his new pens.

Initially, he sold out of the back of a cigar shop but, after a year, word had spread about the quality of his products. Coupled with a five-year guarantee his pens became the ones to have if you wanted quality writing tools. Advertising in popular magazines ensured the orders came rolling in. Just before the start of the twentieth century, he opened a factory in Montreal and had increased the number of designs offered.

The late 1900s was a busy time for another manufacturer of fountain pens. In Philadelphia, a man named Purvis was striving to develop an inexpensive and more durable version of the fountain pen. By placing an elastic tube between the nib and the reservoir, he enabled the ink to return to the barrel by way of suction. This lessened the chance of spills and also increased the length of life of the ink. His adaptions introduced the fountain pen to the man on the street as it became much more affordable to the working classes.

Other fountain pen improvements

When the 20th century began, the world of fountain pens really exploded. Numerous patents were issued and the improvements in the writing quality of pens rocketed. The real progress, however, was in the field of self-filling designs. Below, you will find listed a number of these innovations and explanations as to how they worked.

- **The Button Filler**: Parker pens were the first brand to offer this method of ink filling in 1913. A button on the outside of the pen flattened the ink sac within and allowed the ink to flow through the nib.
- **Level Filler**: This method went on to become the most popular way to fill a pen for the best part of the forty years that followed its introduction in 1912. The external lever lay flat against the pen when not in use but, when lifted, it depressed the internal ink storage and reflated it when the nib was in the Inkwell.
- **Click Filler**: For this method, two protruding tabs were used to deflate the ink sac in the same way as the button and lever fillers but, because they made a distinct clicking sound, the name stuck.
- **The Matchstick Filler**: Introduced in 1910 by the Weidlich manufacturers, there was a small hole in the barrel of the pen that allowed the user to deflate the ink sac with a customized stick. The name derived from the fact that if the user mislaid his stick, a simple matchstick could replace it.
- **The Coin Filler**: This was produced by Waterman to compete with the highly successful lever filler that was patented by Schaeffer. In the same manner as the coin filler, a slot in the barrel enabled the writer to insert a coin to deflate the sac.

Gold nibs were popular at the time as inks corroded steel nibs, but the material proved too soft for successful longevity. Iridium replaced the gold eventually and became the popular metal for fountain pen brands.

Owning a fountain pen was a labor of love at the time. Once they had purchased their pen, the owner would engrave his initials on the clip to discourage other users from taking it. It took months to break a new pen in as nibs were designed to react to pressure and allow the writer to experiment with the width of his strokes. Every nib became accustomed to its owner's style and, if someone else used your pen, it could undo months of work.

The introduction of the ink cartridge in the 1950s was a huge success and enabled the ordinary user to change their ink in a quick and mess-free way. This should have been the invention that saw the fountain pen enter every home, but it was completely eclipsed by the invention of the ballpoint pen.

This convenient, throwaway pen became the darling of the office world and could be seen in the hands of lowly secretaries to managing directors. The school system also saw the benefits of ditching the fountain pen and embraced the new innovative way to put pen to paper.

These days, people see fountain pens as classic writing tools and it is a niche way to write, but the enthusiasts in the field are passionate about their pens. There is a growing choice of pens out there and, for the real enthusiasts, the chance to get their hands on an original model cannot be passed up. Working pens dating back to the time that Waterman blotted his contract are hot collectibles and are sought after items.

Chapter Two: Your First Fountain Pen

Selecting your first pen involves many considerations including the size of your hand, the writing you are doing and the size of your handwriting.

Imagine you are buying a new watch. Is it for practical purposes such as sports? Is it a dress watch you need or a day to day watch that meets all your needs? There are many variants to consider and these are some of the more obvious ones.

Hand Size

If your pen is unsuitable for your hand you will experience fatigue and possible damage to your muscles. If you have large hands, then pick a pen with a barrel that is substantial and a pen that is longer. Smaller hands will benefit from shorter barrels and smaller pens, as these models often incorporate contoured grips that allow a smaller hand to maintain the hold. There is a model called the "Lilliput" that is merely five inches in length when posted (cap on) and is a great option for tiny hands.

Characters

Asian scripts such as Chinese and Japanese contain minute details that are written in very thin lines to aid legibility. If you need to write intricate characters you will need to choose a fine nib, or even extra fine if you are thinking about calligraphy. Traditionally, you would need a nib that allows you to lift your pen from the paper regularly.

The western script has relatively simple shapes and can be enhanced with a broader nib. Western writers also use a style that is known as cursive and using this style allows the writing to flow faster as it does not require lifting the pen. If you do pick a broad nib, be aware that you run a greater risk of ink pooling and bleeding.

Handwriting size

The general guide suggests that the smaller your handwriting, the finer the nib you need. As with hand size, the larger your script, the broader your nib should be. Small writing with a broad nib will look squashed and illegible while larger writing with a fine nib will appear spidery and out of proportion.

Popular Western style brands include Parker, Monteverde, Lamy and Kaweco.

Popular Japanese brands include Pilot and Sailor.

Budget Concerns? Try the Preppy!

Are you just testing the water as far as fountain pens are concerned? Do you want to experience the pleasure of writing with a fountain pen but don't want to spend a large sum of money? There is a brand that will allow you to try out a fountain pen for the price of a cup of coffee. The Platinum Preppy is a fun demonstrator pen that looks, at first glance, like a cheap rollerball pen.

The preppy has a clear plastic body that shows you all the mechanics inside. The springs, the cartridge, you can watch the ink flow to the nib. The Preppy also has a clear cap that you can see the plain steel nib. This pen writes so smoothly you will be tempted to use it on every surface possible, great for beginners who are a little bit nervous regarding usage.

The looks leave a lot to be desired, but functionality is a major plus factor when considering your first purchase. This pen is a great introduction to the world of fountain pens for around ten dollars.

Going up a level

If you are ready to up your budget slightly, then this is where the fun begins! Pens in the next price range have more features to choose from and offer a wider choice. Choose a pen that has the body that suits your style and hand size. Pens in this range can also include converters that are more economical than cartridges. The Pilot range includes the Metropolitan that can allow you to interchange nibs depending on your needs. Pilot is a respected brand and a natural choice to take you to the next step.

If you are having trouble with your grip and find it difficult to maintain the position you need to write smoothly, then consider the Lamy range of fountain pens. The Safari, in particular, has contoured grips that allow the user to write more comfortably. These pens also come in fun colors and are constructed from the same material as Lego blocks. Bright and cheerful colors combined with indestructible material make this a choice for daily use.

These pens can be purchased for less than twenty dollars and all models have a large range of accessories that can be used to enhance your writing.

Next level pens

Fancy a pen with a built-in piston mechanism that fills your pen cleanly and simply? It sounds like it could cost a pretty penny, right? Well, you can have this option for only thirty dollars or so! Try the Diamond range of pens that has a clear plastic body allowing you to see the inner mechanisms and ink supply. This level pen will also encourage you to service your pens yourself. The design will allow you to completely take your pen apart and reassemble it with ease. Certain models also come equipped with tools and grease to help you maintain your new pen. Some of the designs also have a cap that cannot be posted. Look out for the design that suits you best.

The sky is the limit

If you do become a fountain pen aficionado, you now have many levels of pens to choose from. Specialty pens can include the Lilliput that we mentioned earlier if you have started to use your pen regularly and struggle to post your pen why not choose a cap less pen? These pens allow you to whip them out and jot stuff down when the inspiration strikes!

Have you started to use your pen at work? Be aware that you will be judged on your choice of writing implement as you are on your outfit choice. Choose a classic business model that will not look out of place in the White House. Kaweco has pens that fit the bill for around the hundred-dollar mark.

These are just a few suggestions to help you purchase the pen that is right for you. Have fun exploring all the different options and choose your pen well!

Chapter Three: Fountain Pen Filling Systems Explained

There are several ways to fill your pen with ink and, in this chapter, we will examine the different methods and their pros and cons. This will help you decide the type of pen you will purchase.

Cartridge

The cartridge is a tube-shaped reservoir of ink and is the easiest option available. To install a cartridge, follow these simple steps

- Press the stopper into the pens grip section. The stopper is the part of the cartridge that is slightly narrower than the main body.
- Apply gentle force to the cartridge until the stopper is punctured, you will both feel and hear a gentle pop once the cartridge is inserted correctly.
- Place your pen in a downward position to allow the ink to travel to the nib.

Pros of the cartridge system

- Simplicity: You can pop in a new cartridge in a matter of seconds.
- Convenience: Cartridges are lightweight and portable. If you are traveling with your pen and likely to run out of ink outside the office or home, then you avoid having to carry bottled ink.
- Price: This is the cheapest way to fill your pen and cartridges are readily available in shops, unlike ink, which must be purchased in specialty outlets.

Cons of the cartridge system

- Lack of choice: Cartridges differ slightly depending on the make of your pen. Typically, you will be limited to your choice of cartridge depending on the brand of pen you use. This can mean you are restricted with your choice of colors.
- Quality: Bottled inks come in a range of quality, which cartridges don't. *Quick Tip:* you can use a blunt syringe to fill spent cartridges with quality inks.
- Capacity: The cartridge has the smallest capacity of all the systems and will require more changes.

Converter Cartridge

The converter method uses force to draw ink into the pen through the nib. There are two types of converters that use slightly different actions to create the flow of ink to the pen. These are the piston converters and the squeeze converter. Here are instructions on the installation of both.

How to install a piston converter

- Insert the converter into the pen in the same manner as you would a cartridge.
- Place the nib into the ink bottle
- Twist the knob at the end of the converter until it is extended fully.
- Turn the piston in the other direction and this will cause the ink to flow into the chamber.
- Repeat until the converter is full.

How to install a squeeze converter

- Insert the converter into the pen as you would when using a cartridge.
- Place the nib into the ink bottle
- Squeeze the chamber until bubbles appear in the ink.
- Decrease pressure on the converter slowly, the change in pressure will cause the ink to draw into the pen.
- Squeeze and repeat until the ink is free from bubbles. This signals that your converter is full.

Pros of a converter

- Diversity: Many cartridge pens allow the use of a converter.
- Quality: Converters allow a wider use of premier inks.

Cons of a converter

- Compatibility: As with cartridges, different brands are not always compatible. Check both your pen and the converter before any purchase.
- Capacity: Many converters are smaller than the barrel of the pen and only hold as much ink as a cartridge. This often means that when you are outside the office or home, you will need access to an inkbottle. This is not always practical and can be messy.

Built-in filling systems

When you are shopping for pens, you will come across some models that have a system already in place. This allows you to simply dip your pen into the inkbottle and fill. There are two types of systems that are incorporated into the pen and here are the instructions for both the piston filler and the vacuum filling system.

How to use a built-in piston filling system

- Begin by submerging the whole of the nib into the ink, unlike the converter, you must submerge the entire nib.
- Twist the end of the pen until the piston is at full capacity.
- Turning the knob in the opposite direction will cause the piston action to retract. This allows the ink to be drawn into the container. Your pen should fill after the first action but if it does not repeat the motion until full capacity is achieved.

How to use a built-in vacuum filling system

- Unscrew the end of your pen and you will see a plunger. Pull this back until it is fully extended.
- Slowly push the plunger back into the chamber.
- Submerge the nib and pull it back into the pen. This action will cause the ink to fill the container.

Pros of the built-in systems

- Capacity: These inbuilt systems hold significantly more ink than cartridge or converters as the whole barrel is used to contain ink.

- Quality: These systems allow you to explore the whole range of quality inks that are available.

Cons of the built-in systems

- Adaptability - Once you have chosen an inbuilt system you are stuck with it. It is not an option to convert to cartridge or converter options.
- Price: These types of pens are inevitably more expensive than pens with the simpler systems.

Eyedropper pens

As the name suggests, an eyedropper pen involves filling the barrel with a separate instrument. You can use an eyedropper, obviously, or a blunt-edged syringe. This is one of the earliest methods used to fill a pen and appeals to people who appreciate the history of the fountain pen. Many eyedropper pens are converted from cartridge pens to increase ink capacity.

How to fill an eyedropper pen

- Open the fountain pen barrel by unscrewing the end of your pen.
- Use silicone grease to coat the grip section of your pen. Ensure the threads are covered completely or your pen will leak.
- Once you have created a watertight seal take your chosen instrument and fill the barrel until the ink reaches the threads of your grip section.

Pros of an eyedropper pen

- Capacity: The whole barrel is filled with ink and this ensures your pen needs filling less often than cartridge or converter pens.
- Choice: You can fill your pen with all the different quality inks available.

Cons of an eyedropper pen

- Leaks: This system is prone to messiness if the barrel is not watertight or you misjudge with your eyedropper. Involving separate components makes the whole process more prone to leaks.
- Inconvenient: You not only have to travel with an inkbottle, but you must also have silicone grease and your chosen filling method with you. This is not ideal when you are away traveling or in a rush to write.

Quick note: Not all cartridge pens are suitable for conversion to eyedropper pens. Check there are no exposed metallic elements in the barrel and make sure the barrel is airtight before attempting to convert your pen.

Chapter Four: How to Write with a Fountain Pen and How the Pen Works

At one time, penmanship was taught in schools at an early age. Today, we are all familiar with ballpoint pens and expect the same quality of writing from different angles and hand positions. Fountain pens require a little more finesse and, in this chapter, we will describe how to hold the pen properly and use the correct pressure. Experiment with different adjustments to create a smooth and comfortable writing style that suits you.

Get a Grip

Post or no post: Before you begin to write, you may want to address the cap of your pen. Attaching it to the pen (posting) can make your pen feel more balanced, but if your hand is small, you may prefer to leave the cap off (no post).

You are now ready to hold your pen in the correct position. Hold the pen between your thumb and index finger. The barrel of your pen should now be resting on the last knuckle of your middle finger. The remaining two fingers, along with the edge of your hand, should now be resting on your writing surface and should feel secure enough to provide stability. Your pen should now be forming a forty-five-degree angle away from your paper, give or take five degrees either way. This is known as the "sweet spot" of your nib. You may find the position is lower than your normal writing position, but it is necessary to allow a smooth ink flow to your nib.

If you are finding this position is causing you strain on your finger you can adjust the pen to a higher position. Using an easel-like grip can ease the strain but will take some practice.

The Sweet Spot

Your nib has a tip that is made up of tines and feed. Once you find the position of your nib that allows you to write smoothly and with continuity. The ink should be flowing freely, and the writing should not feel scratchy. Your pen should not experience skipping but should flow easily. This is your "sweet spot" and you will learn to find it with practice.

Use your Arm

A common mistake among fountain pen novices is to write without moving their hand. Using their fingers to flex and control the pen can be exhausting and can lead to a serious strain of the digits! The chances of maintaining the "sweet spot" are also reduced so what is the answer?

Maintain the "sweet spot" and avoid injury to your fingers by using the whole of your lower arm to propel your pen. The muscles in your arm are larger and more developed than your hand and can cope with maintaining height and rotation, ensuring you are more comfortable when writing.

Under Pressure

If you are a regular user or ballpoint pens, you will be used to applying pressure in order to write. Fountain pens do not require the same amount of pressure, so you must ignore your natural instinct to apply tension to you your pen. Allow the nib to glide across the paper and your job is to guide it to form your script. Applying too much pressure can also damage your nib and misalign it.

It may help you to write better if you understand the mechanism of your pen so here are the different components of your fountain pen.

- The Nib: This is the iconic part of the pen and consists of a metal pointed piece that draws ink into the pen using capillary action. The two halves of the nib are called tines. They surround the ink slit and are coated with hard metal to avoid wearing out.
- The Feed: This is the part of the pen that sits beneath the nib and supplies the flow of ink to it. The feed can often have fins that help regulate this flow but are only seen when the pen is dismantled. The feed will only work if it is sitting directly under the nib and it needs to be free of any obstruction to work optimally. Always use approved fountain pen ink as ordinary ink can contain binding agents that will clog up your feed and may destroy this integral part of your pen.
- Ink supply: This is the part of the pen that distinguishes it from a dip pen. Traditional dip pens used an external ink supply, normally in the form of a well but fountain pens have an internal reservoir. Some pens have simple cartridges that hold a certain amount of ink while others have a converter that allows ink to be sucked in from a bottle.
- The cap: There are a few types of pen that retract, but the majority has caps to prevent the nib drying out. Whenever the pen is not in use, the cap should be replaced securely as your pen can dry up in minutes if left open.
- The section: The core of your pen the section holds the nib and the feed together forming a single nib unit. This allows for easier cleaning and can also be

replaced easily as it is a part that may sustain damage.

- Barrel: This is the part of the pen that contains the section and is the part of the pen that can be customized to fit your style. For most pens, it is simply a shell that protects the inner working parts of your pen but, with eyedropper pens, the barrel is the ink dispenser.

Now you know how your pen works imagine the ink flowing through the different components as it reaches your nib. This can help you write with a more flowing style and embrace the beauty of your fountain pen. There is an artistry to the makeup of your writing tool and the more you appreciate it, the better you will write.

CHAPTER FIVE: HOW TO CLEAN AND MAINTAIN A FOUNTAIN PEN

Your pen is a well-tuned machine and, as such, requires cleaning and maintenance. When a pen is being used on a regular basis, debris will collect in the nib and feed which will clog the action and cause the pen to perform below par. Dust and fibers in the atmosphere will combine with dried flakes of ink to block the capillary action.

Symptoms that a pen requires cleaning are uneven ink flow and scratching. The pen may also tend to skip when writing. Standard times for cleaning are around every six weeks, even if the pen is writing well, and the pen should be cleaned every time you change ink.

Depending on usage and age of the pen there are different types of cleaning and the procedures are explained below.

1) **The simple clean**: This clean is sufficient if the pen is writing well and there is no ink change.

   - Dismantle the pen: Uncap the pen and remove the section that contains the nib from the main barrel of the pen. If the pen has a cartridge or an alternative ink container, then it should be removed at the same time as the nib. If you want to save the ink and reuse it use sticky tape to seal the vessel and avoid the ink evaporating.
   - Rinse: Under a running tap, rinse the nib section for twenty seconds to remove the

detachable debris and make the next step simpler. Always use cold or tepid water as hot water will damage the pen.

- Immerse: Fill a see-through container with cold water and place the nib into it, ensuring it is covered completely. Leave to soak until the water is stained with ink. Replace with more clean water and repeat until the water is clear. Once you have clear water, leave the nib in for at least an hour and then your clean is complete. Regular tap water works well, but if you have a high mineral content you may wish to use distilled water. There is no standard amount of times you will have to change the water as different inks have higher saturation levels.

- Dry: You now need to dry out the nib for at least ten hours and, if possible, leave it a full day. Wrap the nib in a paper towel and leave it nib down in a small jug or glass. The paper towel will help to draw out the water from within the nib.

- Restore: Once dry you may reinstall your cartridge and assemble your pen.

2) **Full flushing**: This method should be used when the pen is writing poorly, or an ink change is required.

- Rinsing: Follow steps one and two of the simple clean to remove flakes of ink.

- Flush: Use a container half filled with cold, clean water and place your cartridge into the liquid, draw the water into the vessel and squeeze to empty. Repeat this procedure until the water is clear.

- Reattach: Take the cartridge and affix it to the nib section and place the nib in a vessel with cold, clean water.

- Clean: In the same manner as you cleaned the cartridge, use it to draw water into your nib section until the water is ink free.

- Soak: Leave in clean water for two hours to ensure that all traces of ink are gone.

- Dry and rebuild: Follow the final steps of the simple clean to complete the procedure.

If your pen is still showing traces of old ink, then you may have to invest in some commercial cleaning solutions. Sometimes water just isn't enough and there are a number of solutions available. When using a cleaning aid, add a few drops when soaking the nib. Different manufacturers recommend varying amounts of time to soak your nib and these instructions should be adhered to whenever possible. Take extra care when rinsing your pen as cleaning solution will affect the performance of your pen.

Homemade Cleaning solutions

You can always take some household cleaners and use them to clean your fountain pen providing you follow some simple tips.

- Dish soap: Just a couple of drops in your water will provide an effective cleaner for your pen, too much will make flushing more difficult.

- Ammonia: If your pen is not responding to gentle cleaning you can use this recipe to make a stronger solution, do not use to clean aluminum, brass or copper nibs as corrosion can occur.

10 parts distilled water
1-part ammonia
Two drops of dish soap
Combine in a jar, shake and add to cleaning water.

- Bleach: If all else fails, you can use a diluted bleach solution to clean your pen. This should only be used as a last resort as bleach can damage your pen beyond repair.

Never mix bleach and ammonia as they create a toxic vapor that can be harmful.

3) Advanced Nib cleaning: With some pens, it is possible to disassemble the nib to allow a comprehensive cleaning procedure. Take note that this procedure may void your warranty depending on the manufacturer. Always take care when disassembling your nib and treat it gently. The majority of pens will allow you to remove the nib simply by pulling, this will leave you with three sections that can all be cleaned separately and left to dry. Some pens will have a screw in nib section and you need to unscrew the whole unit first to prevent damage to the thread.

If you follow these cleaning tips, it is possible your pen can last you a lifetime, the time and effort to care for your pen will be rewarded by the quality of your writing. Another important tip to maintain the quality of your pen is to never lend your pen to anyone else. The nib of your pen will gently customize to your style of writing and your hand and pen strokes. Allowing someone else to use your pen will result in it becoming maladjusted and will result in serious repairs that will need specialist attention.

Chapter Six: The Best Paper to Compliment your Fountain Pen

Your choice of paper for your fountain pen is as important as choosing the right wine to compliment a meal. The different combinations allow the tastes and subtleties to pair together and provide the ultimate experience. In the same way, the correct paper for your fountain pen adds another dimension to your writing experience. There are many factors to consider when choosing your perfect paper and, in this chapter, we will consider the choices that you must make to ensure you have the premium paper for your personal style.

Color of paper

White is the seemingly obvious choice, right? A crisp, clean white paper will enhance the colors of your ink and highlight your text beautifully. There is an alternative color that you may want to consider if you are looking for an effect that is easier on the eye. The rich cream colored paper is available in a fountain pen friendly form and can add a touch of style to your writing. Imagine the joy of opening a handwritten invitation on cream paper with flowing ink strokes from your fountain pen, special occasions would be made even more memorable with a simple choice of paper.

Feathering

This is the effect created when ink spreads through a paper's fiber and creates a feather-like effect at the edge of your writing. Low-quality paper is more prone to feathering but what happens when you are still feathering on high-quality paper? It could be your nib or the viscosity of your ink. Choose high-quality paper that is designed to resist the spreading of ink. High fiber content will help you write clearly and without a web-like mess marring your script.

Bleed through

Bleed through is when you can see traces of what you have written on the other side of your paper. Fountain pen paper is designed specifically to avoid bleed through but, if it occurs, you may need to check your nib. It could be that your nib is overloading with ink and needs attention. To avoid bleed-through completely, you should buy the thicker paper.

Drying time

Generally, your drying time is dictated by a combination of ink formula and paper absorbency. However, there can be a downside to your super absorbent paper. There is a direct correlation that links the absorbency of paper to the smoothness of the paper. The more absorbent the paper, the rougher the writing surface. You need to decide what the most important factor is when you are writing. Do you need to have a quick drying paper, or can you wait and use smoother writing paper? Choose a balance between the two that suits you best.

Sheet Style

Like regular paper, fountain pen paper is available in a variety of styles. Blank paper lined, or grid paper are all options to consider. Grid paper has light gray dots forming a grid pattern across the paper, which allow the writer to follow guidelines without having lines upon the paper. This is less obtrusive than lined paper, but if you really prefer blank paper, it can be used with a template that you place behind the paper. This allows you to write between the lines without the actual lines.

Coated paper

The fully coated paper is the smoothest form of fountain pen paper available and it aids the flow of the pen beautifully. However, the surface of the paper is slippery, and the ink lies on top of it and takes a while to dry. Uncoated paper is often too rough to aid smooth writing, and this is known as "toothy" paper. The nib often catches on the rough parts of the paper and makes the writing messy. Generally, a paper that is half coated will give you a smooth writing experience along with an acceptable drying time.

Price

It is a given that paper designed for fountain pens is going to be more expensive than standard paper. This does not mean you have to break the bank when choosing your writing surface and there are a number of suggestions below for paper types and the qualities they offer.

Suggestions for your fountain pen paper

The papers below are rated for your information. Smoothness is on a scale of one to five, with five being superb. Show through is also rated on a one to five ratio with five being the highest amount of show through.

Midori Color Notebook

This brand of notebook offers quality paper with a satin-like finish that allows a smooth flowing writing style. The colored pages are made up of beautifully subtle hues that are unusual in fountain pen paper choice and are one of the more affordable choices. There is significant show through, so the pages can only be used on one side.

Color: Multiple

Smoothness: four

Dry time: twenty seconds

Show through: five

Sheet Style: Lined

Rhodia Dot Paper

Featuring a grid pattern that is easy to follow, this quality paper allows you to write neatly without the paper being intrusive with your style. The low level of show through allows the writer to utilize both sides of the paper.

Color: White

Smoothness: four

Dry time: ten seconds

Show through: one

Sheet style: Dot Grid

Tomoe River paper

This is a thin paper that is impressively high quality. Its velvety surface is a joy to write on and it is highly resistant to bleed through allowing your writing to flow smoothly and cleanly. The lightweight quality of this paper makes it a firm favorite among users who need a thinner, lighter paper.

Color: White or cream

Smoothness: two

Dry time: twenty seconds

Show through: five

Sheet Style: Blank

Pilot letter pad for fountain pens

This notebook paper has wide spaced lines that allow ample space for jottings and notes to remind you of specifics. Its surface is specifically designed to allow smooth writing with a fountain pen and the quality of the paper is so good you can also use the sheets to send special items. Letters or invitations look great on this paper. It has a soft white color that makes it easy on the eye and is a pleasure to look at.

Color: White

Smoothness: five

Dry time: twelve seconds

Show through: one

Sheet Style: Lined

Life vermillion notebook

Easy on the eye, this quality notebook will allow you to use it as an everyday notebook that looks great, allows quality writing and comes in a great range of sizes and sheet styles to suit your needs.

Color: Cream

Smoothness: four

Dry time: fifteen seconds

Show through: two

Sheet Style: Blank, graph, lined.

Choosing your favorite brand of paper can be a daunting process. The papers above were chosen to give you one option from several different categories. There are specialist shops that can offer advice and help you pick the brand that compliments your style. Be aware that buying these stylish notebooks and paper can become addictive. However, there is help out there for stationery junkies!

Share your experiences and pick up helpful tips from social media. There are some dedicated groups on Facebook including a fountain pen hospital and other groups that love to talk about their fountain pens. No matter what your budget, you can join these enthusiasts in their love of all things stationery, find bargain buys for your pen, ink and paper needs.

FAREWELL

And so, dear reader, I bid you farewell.

No doubt, you will be off to the stationery shop as soon as you can. Good luck with your new hobby and happy writing!

My hope is that you use the information in this book to help select, care for, and enjoy your pen to its fullest.

Slow down and enjoy creating your message!

ABOUT THE AUTHOR

HARRISON WEST is famous in some parts of the world and infamous in others.

Mr. West enjoys cigars, alcohol, old books, and new friends...along with slowly crafting messages with exotic pens. (His pen is the one on the cover of this work.)

He resides in smoky rooms with overstuffed leather chairs, book-lined shelves, and dark, heavy, wood furniture.

As I complete this ABOUT section, he is slowly picking up his favorite pen to scrawl the last few words of this book.

Moments later, he looked at me expectantly as if to say: "Why haven't you typed this out yet?"

He made me write this ABOUT page in this way because, he says, he's "not a sharer". Then he laughed deeply, puffed his cigar, and took a long drink of a straight dark rum.

Can't argue with that I guess.

OTHER BOOKS BY HARRISON WEST

Masculine Cocktails: And Where I Found Them

These manly cocktails help make incredible memories. Take a minute, unplug, and discover this unique collection of cocktails that are intriguing, masculine, and available at the local bar or the most upscale pub. Put down the rum & coke and pick up these unique cocktails along with the stories they help make.

The Cigar Cutter: A Beginner's Guide To Selecting The Best Cigars & Cutting The Rest

SELECT THE BEST CIGAR FOR YOU & ENJOY YOUR CIGAR EXPERIENCE!

Wrappers, sizes, colors...there is LOTS to know about cigars. And each choice will impact your enjoyment. Did you know just how much cigar sizes vary from brand to brand? Do you know what color and packing you'll like? Take a look inside and get to know exactly what cigar will work for you.

>>> AVOID A BAD CHOICE

This book teaches you how to select something you'll like. Start getting to know cigars and avoid the coughing spells that come when you select something wrong for you early on!

>>> CONCISE AND CLEAR

The Cigar Cutter walks you through cigar basics quickly and briefly...it keeps things easy for you to get to know cigars and to get you to the fun!

>>> DON'T GET LEFT BEHIND

Cigars are popular for their flavor, mystery, and the ambience they create. Learn about cigars today and pick up on the trend!

How To Unplug From Social Media Freaks: A Beginner's Guide To Breaking Social Media Addiction

SOCIAL MEDIA IS EVERYWHERE...AND HERE'S HOW TO ESCAPE IT!

TAKE BACK YOUR LIFE AND TIME.

Remember last time you celebrated a birthday? Well my friend Sharron didn't. In fact, she didn't remember that much of any of her great moments.

Why? Because she was addicted.

When her phone beeped or lit up, she immediately grabbed for it. And it was tough to live life that way.

I mean, it looked like she was living life the whole time. After all, Instagram and Facebook were filled with photos of what she ate, where she went, and who she was with. Things looked fine.

The problem? They weren't fine at all. She felt lonelier than ever in a sea of social media.

It's easy to wind up that way, and lots of friends tell me so. And when Sharron found out that I write, she asked me to help.

So this one is for Sharron, but more importantly, it's for me too: it's so that I can keep all my friends here, with me, in the real world""living life together.

So I offer you this: use this work to unplug...before it's too late and YOU start forgetting your last great birthday party or that date with a special someone!

>>> AVOID AWKWARD SOCIAL SITUATIONS

A poorly timed phone check or facebook like can kill the mood at a social event. Saying "uh-huh" while swiping at your phone is the surest way to lose a client, a lover, or yourself. Take a look inside for techniques to decrease the poorly timed phone check!

>>> LEARN VALUABLE TECHNIQUES TO UNPLUG

The last time your spouse glared at you for staring at your phone, you may have thought about just how valuable it would be to decrease your social media use. And remember, the social media platforms are DESIGNED to be addicting! Take a look inside to break that difficult cycle of addiction.

>>> RECLAIM YOUR LIFE AND TIME

You get one thing in life, really: your time. Control your devices by controlling your attention and you will reclaim your time. Open up this book to begin reclaiming your life and time from the grip of social media!

ONE LAST THING...

If this book was useful to you or if you enjoyed it, I'd really appreciate your review on Amazon. The support is really important and I do read each and every review so that this work can be updated and improved.

If you're reading the paperback version of the book, I'd appreciate your comments on Amazon.com.

If you're reading this on Kindle, Amazon will ask you for a review. (In just a moment.)

If you enjoyed the book, please take a moment and pass along your feedback!

Printed in Dunstable, United Kingdom

75401498R00031